ONE DIRECTION

THE ULTIMATE PHOTO COLLECTION

ONE DIRECTION

THE ULTIMATE PHOTO COLLECTION

SARAH-LOUISE JAMES

CARLTON
BOOKS

CONTENTS

INTRODUCTION

One Direction need no introduction. Zayn Malik, Harry Styles, Niall Horan, Liam Payne and Louis Tomlinson have gone from *X Factor* hopefuls to global pop superstars in the space of a few short years. They've sold millions of records around the globe, scored two international No. 1 albums, secured a string of No. 1 singles, and have notched up a sell-out worldwide tour. Their legion of devoted fans, the "Directioners", have cheered the boys on all the way: from racking up BRIT Awards and MTV VMAs to becoming Guinness World Record holders after their breakthrough album debuted at the top of the US album charts. It's a feat that no other British act has ever managed – not even The Beatles. There's no stopping One Direction.

IN THE BEGINNING

Above: Lapping up the applause at Hall Cross School in Doncaster. **Right:** Now that's magic. At the Harry Potter world film premiere in London, 2011.

Imagine a world without 1D. However, officially, 1D
were never meant to be. The story goes: Zayn, Liam,
Louis, Harry and Niall all turned up to the 2010 *X Factor*
auditions to try their luck as solo singers – but none of
them made the final cut. Fortunately, *X Factor* supremo
Simon Cowell and his panel pal Nicole Scherzinger
could see their potential and decided to channel
their talents in a new direction. One Direction!

Above: Hanging out in their onesies during the *X Factor* days, 2010. **Bottom and right:** The boys hanging out in the *X Factor* studios in London in 2010.

When *X Factor* boss Simon Cowell asked the lads if they wanted to form a band, they bit his hand off. Together, they weren't just good, they were magic. They went from plucky solo hopefuls to one of the most popular acts in the competition. As the boys progressed through the *X Factor*, they amassed more and more of a following – fans who would turn up early to the TV studios just to scrrrreeeeeeeeeam.

Top left: On the *X Factor* campaign trail in 2010.
Bottom left and above: Suited and booted at a movie premiere in London.

The lads on the iconic zebra crossing outside the Abbey Road Studios, home of The Beatles' most famous recordings.

Blue-eyed, blonde-haired Niall Horan easily pulls off the rock-star look as he performs at a 1D concert in 2013. Born in Mullingar, Ireland, in 1993, Horan has been playing guitar since his childhood.

NIALL

Irish lad Niall isn't the youngest member of the band (he was born before Harry) but he's the band member the others like to mother the most! "There is no doubt Niall is the cute one," says Louis. Those baby blues and the adorable Irish accent make him hard to resist.

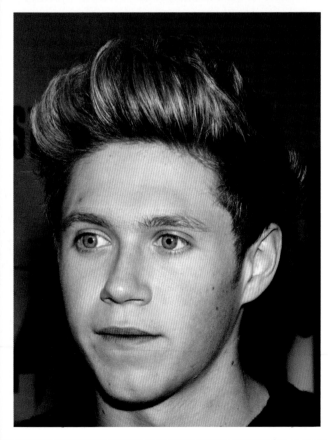

Niall says he's always "lived and breathed music". As soon as he could join the school choir he did, and when he received a guitar at the tender age of four there was no looking back. It's no surprise this mix of talent and determination won him a place in 1D. His winning Irish charm has made him a fan fave, too, and on US tours the loudest screams are usually for Niall. Niall was chuffed to discover that his 1D doll was the biggest seller on Amazon at the end of 2012!

Niall having fun posing for his Madame Tussauds wax model in 2013. Let's hope they capture his blue eyes, blonde hair and gorgeous good looks.

Niall's good looks have not gone unnoticed by celebrity ladies and the Irish boy has been linked with A-list celebrities.

Life in 1D is a whirlwind and Niall loves every minute of it. He says, "Our life is like an extended *Inbetweeners* movie. There are not many 18-year-old fellas who can say they've travelled the world, so it's pretty crazy. We get a lot of attention from female fans and we have to be careful not to get in trouble." Despite the attention, Niall has admitted he's not ready for a relationship just yet. Directioners, you're all still in with a chance!

On being on stage, Niall says, "I love it. I love the screaming. They love it, too: they've all got their tickets and they've been waiting a year or so to see you, so you've got to give it your best."

In the space of a few years, Mullingar boy Niall has gone from regular teenage lad to global heart-throb. He and the rest of the boys are greeted with scenes of hysteria wherever they go. Niall recalls one time when the lads were chased while touring in the States: "We were heading out to go to a concert and we turned the corner from our hotel and all the girls started running down the main avenue after us. It was like something out of a zombie movie."

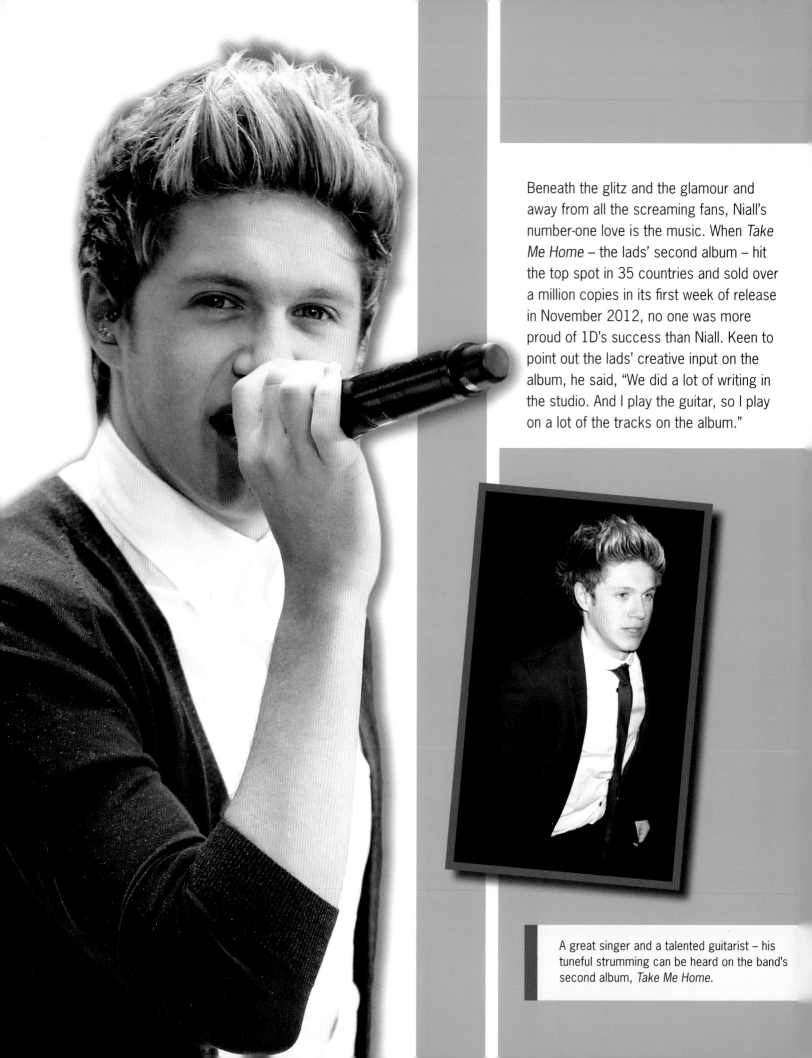

Beneath the glitz and the glamour and away from all the screaming fans, Niall's number-one love is the music. When *Take Me Home* – the lads' second album – hit the top spot in 35 countries and sold over a million copies in its first week of release in November 2012, no one was more proud of 1D's success than Niall. Keen to point out the lads' creative input on the album, he said, "We did a lot of writing in the studio. And I play the guitar, so I play on a lot of the tracks on the album."

A great singer and a talented guitarist – his tuneful strumming can be heard on the band's second album, *Take Me Home*.

THE START OF SOMETHING SPECIAL

Above: The lads lap up the screams on tour in Birmingham. **Right:** On top of the world: at the Real Radio Awards in Manchester in August in 2011.

Simon Cowell knew that 1D were the real winners of *X Factor* 2010 and no sooner had the show finished than he signed them up to his record label Syco in a megabucks deal. New Year 2011 got off to an amazing start for Liam, Zayn, Niall, Louis and Harry as the lads were whisked off to LA to record their debut album.

It was busy, busy, busy in 2011. In February the lads embarked on the *X Factor* Live Tour and by the time the gigs wrapped in April – and they'd played to more than half a million fans up and down the UK – there was no question who the loudest screams were for.

Left: Performing at Heaven Nightclub in London.
Top: At the Capital FM Jingle Bell Ball in 2011. **Below:**
Looking suave at the *GQ Magazine* Awards in 2011.

At a record signing at HMV on Oxford Street, London, in September 2011. The boys certainly look happy to be there.

1D released their debut single, "What Makes You Beautiful", in September 2011 and it zoomed to No. 1 in the UK and was named the fastest-selling single of the year. It wasn't just British Directioners who loved the tune, either – "WMYB" topped the charts in Europe, Australia and New Zealand. The single also came to the attention of fans and music executives in the US and in November the lads signed a massive record deal with Columbia Records.

31

Zayn Malik is known as the brooding "bad boy" hunk of 1D – but he's a softie at heart. Zayn's name means "beautiful" in Arabic and we don't think any of his 8 million Twitter followers would disagree.

ZAYN

Thank goodness Simon Cowell persuaded a nervous Zayn not to worry about his dance moves during the X Factor auditions back in 2010. The Bradford-born hottie almost walked off set, never to return. Mr Cowell managed to persuade him to give it another shot. 1D just wouldn't have been the same without Zayn!

Zayn was born in Bradford in 1993 to mum Tricia and dad Yaser and has three sisters. He was always a studious kid and could usually be found with his nose buried in a book. If he hadn't joined 1D, he'd have gone to university to study English. Thankfully for Directioners, the sometimes-shy teen decided to bite the bullet and audition for *X Factor*. The panel saw his potential and now Zayn's is one of the most recognizable faces on the planet.

Zayn looking mean and moody on stage. The Bradford boy loves to write. Expect to see self-penned 1D songs soon!

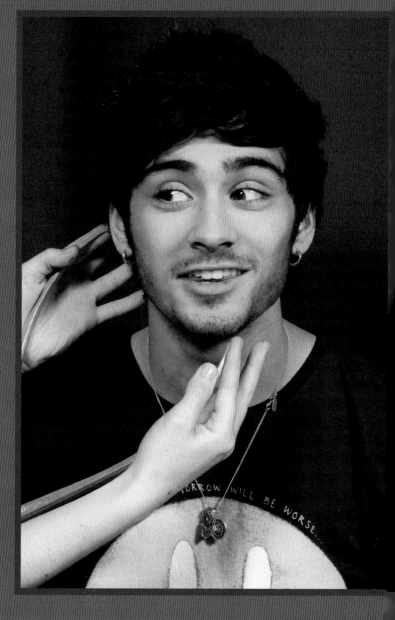

He's got movie-star good looks – chiselled jaw, cool hair, smouldering eyes – so it's no surprise to hear that Zayn cares about his appearance. Whether he's sporting downtime trackie bottoms or living it up in a suit, he always likes to look polished. The other members of the band love to poke fun at him about it, too. Harry says, "We joke about it. We'll say, 'Zayn, quick, look, there's a mirror over there you've missed.'"

Zayn – he's naturally gorgeous, whether he chooses to spend a long time in front of the mirror or not! Here he poses for the cameras at the 2013 BRIT Awards.

Could Zayn get any more ADORABLE?
Um, yep. Here is the 1D hottie performing
with an uber-cute pup on his lap in 2012.

Style-conscious Zayn might stroll through airports after long-haul flights looking ultra cool (with his Louis Vuitton luggage), he might read poetry, take care of his appearance and love puppies, but he likes to be a lad in a boyband. "It's really cool for me because with having three sisters I was used to being around a lot of girls all the time. So to be around lads is really new. I get to just be a lad." Phew, we think – otherwise he'd be too perfect!

Zayn has always had a fondness for the rockabilly look: leather jackets, tight jeans – and the Bradford boy does love rocking a quiff! "Zayn's quiff is almost as tall as Mount Kilimanjaro," Harry once quipped. "We measured it once and it was eight inches." Zayn can also pull off the cool punk look too. Whatever his style or look, Zayn will always be a big hit with Directioners.

One Direction's Zayn performing on stage in full rockabilly mode, with a badger stripe on his quiff.

1-DELIRIUM!

Above: Something's up Down Under. Fans scream for 1D at a concert in Sydney in April 2012. **Right:** 1D share a joke at the Muchmusic studios in Toronto, Canada.

1D fans – AKA the Directioners – span one side of
the globe to the other, from the UK to Australia.
Directioners are loyal, fully paid-up, loved-up members
of the 1D fanclub who'd do anything for their idols.
Fans have gone to extreme lengths to catch a close-up
glimpse of the boys, including one smitten kitten who
hid inside a bin outside one of their concert venues.
Maybe just a li'l bit crazy – but the 1D boys love it!

Deafening screams greet One Direction at the Nickelodeon 25th Annual Kids' Choice Awards in Los Angeles in March 2012.

The lads were propelled to international fame before they'd even released a record. Swathes of lovestruck fans from across the globe watched their videos on YouTube, waited eagerly for their 140-character tweets and followed the lads' progress on Facebook. So, by the time they eventually hit the promo trail for debut album *Up All Night*, the crowds were immense. Wherever they went in the world the boys were faced with hordes and hordes of delirious fans.

Top: On home turf, Harry's hometown of Holmes Chapel to be exact. **Bottom:** Getting up close and personal with the fans at Muchmusic, Canada.

One Direction whip their loyal fans into a frenzy as they kick off their blockbuster *Take Me Home* Tour in London in 2013. The teen idols will perform more than 100 shows around the world.

The boys say they'll never get used to the adulation. "You notice it when you've had a few days off and you go out to the shop and you forget that people recognize your face," says Louis. "You pick up your milk and then someone says, 'Can I have a photo?'" Luckily for Directioners, the boys love nothing more than getting out there and meeting and performing for the fans – not to mention signing autographs, collecting pressies and snatching the odd kiss.

Top left: Liam poses for a fan photograph in London in 2013. **Left:** Fans at the launch of the 1D World store in Calgary in 2013. **Above:** Screams to raise the rooftop, and the 1D boys – at the Radio 1 Teen Awards in London.

1D STYLE

Above: Looking dapper at the Nickelodeon Kids' Choice Awards in March 2012. **Right:** Wrapped up warm at Z100's Jingle Ball in New York in December 2010.

One Direction all have their own specific style. Down-to-earth lads' lad Niall loves nothing more than hanging out in casual jeans and trainers. Zayn loves the Americana look – as his rockabilly quiff proves. Louis has a passion for high-street fashion and can often be seen in the latest styles. Liam's look is classic guy uniform – smart jackets, check shirts and jeans. Harry, meanwhile, loves the preppy look – no one can quite rock a bow-tie like Mr Styles.

Above: Men in black and white at the *Men in Black 3* premiere in 2012. **Right:** Looking super-sleek in navy shades at the *X Factor* Season Finale in LA.

Nineties girlband The Spice Girls all had a nickname, so maybe 1D should too. Based on their fashion choices, Harry can be Preppy D; Zayn, Cool D; Louis, Trendy D; Liam, Classic D; and Niall, Sunny D. "Everyone's style is properly coming through now," says Zayn. "Niall's really cool, casual and chilled out. Liam dresses quite smart. Harry dresses quite preppy. Louis's got his cool, surfer-boy look and I like to add a bit of urban with a bit a rockiness."

Suits you, boys! One Direction looking seriously slick and stylish at the *GQ* Magazine Awards in 2011.

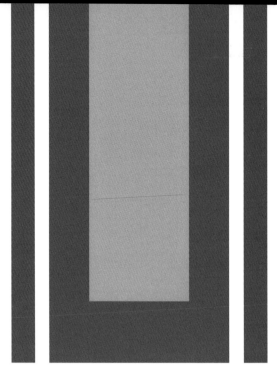

Don't they look smart? 1D might spend a lot of time knocking around in their jeans, tees and trainers, but when the occasion to dress up comes knocking, the lads embrace it with open arms. And boy, do they look handsome when they rock a suit! Their style hasn't gone unnoticed by some of the world's biggest fashion editors either – the band have posed for trendy US mags *Wonderland* and *Teen Vogue*, and British *Vogue*.

Hanging out in coordinated clobber
at the Radio 1 Teen Awards in London
in 2012.

It's usually girls who get a reputation for loving shoes – but OMG do the 1D boys love their sneakers. Especially Zayn, who owns hundreds of pairs. Line all the band's shoes up and they might just "walk" half way around the world. Style maven Harry, meanwhile, perhaps takes fashion the most seriously. Not only does he love hitting fashion shows when they're in town, he also rocks a moody model pose! If you've got it flaunt it, Harry.

Top: Harry looking every part the male model.
Bottom: Who would have thought these shades could work so well? The boys back at the *X Factor* in November 2011.

Adored by millions of Directioners, heart-throb Liam has a winning smile and laid-back ways that make him a firm favourite with the fans and the 1D boys.

LIAM

Chocolate-drop-eyed Liam Payne famously auditioned twice for *X Factor*. In 2008 he was told he was "too young" to proceed through the competition, but the plucky lad came back fighting in 2010. Just as well for all of us Directioners, because he went on to become an integral member of the best band in the world.

No one in the band changes their barnet
as much as he does. He shocked fans
with a buzz cut at the tail end of 2012.

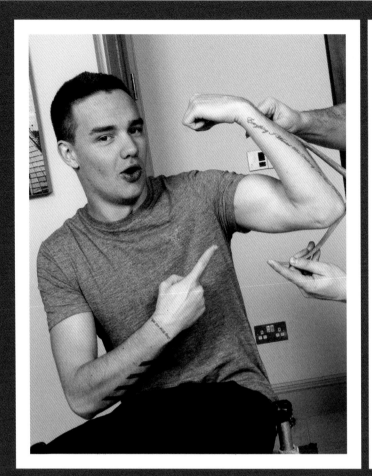

He might be known as the sensible one in 1D, but Liam releases his rebellious streak via an ever-changing array of hairdos – from Harry-style curls, to shaved, to sleek red-carpet style. And his chameleon look means he can lead a private life when he wants to, too. He says, "At the start, management said I wasn't allowed to change my hair. But then I did it anyway, so they kind of let that one go. I tend to change my hair quite a lot."

Liam was born in 1993 to mum and dad Karen and Geoff. He took up boxing and cross-country running as a young teen and was really successful in both sports. He says, "I was bullied by a few people who were much older than me. So I went to camp to learn to box. It gave me confidence to know that if I could fight, I could stand up to anyone." Liam admits he's still quite competitive – but it's this fighting spirit that has seen him take his place in One Direction.

Looking good! He might change his look on a regular basis, but here Liam shows he can smould like a red-carpet hunk with the best of them.

Liam loves joking around as much as the rest of the band and can still summon up a big grin after a gruelling long-haul flight. Perhaps it's because he loves his job so much! Nowadays, Liam steps out on stage and is met with thousands of adoring fans. But it wasn't always that way. His worst-ever singing gig was as a 16-year-old performing at a small festival in Wales. He says, "I played for ten people for £50." He doesn't need to worry any more.

Left: Liam on stage, reaching out to hundreds of adoring fans. **Above:** Liam having a rest after a long-haul flight.

Liam always knew it was his destiny to be a singer and nothing would get in his way – even a 2008 *X Factor* rejection.

Liam and the lads spend their lives touring the globe, singing on stage for fans, making radio hosts laugh during radio interviews, but they never let the fame go to their heads. Liam says, "We never expected anything like this to happen. We thought we might have a record in the UK, maybe, but never come out to America and have a No. 1 album. It's beyond all of our wildest dreams."

1D HAVING FUN!

Above: Zapped! 1D with toy guns at a movie premiere in March 2012. **Right:** It was his birthday, so I suppose Niall's allowed to be naughty and smash a cake in Louis' face.

Without a doubt, 1D have just as much fun off stage as they do on. Whether they're blasting paps with toy guns, as they did at the *Men in Black 3* premiere in NYC in 2012, or shoving birthday cake into each other's faces, the band's mischievous streak is a big part of their appeal. Well, the lads do say they're brothers from another mother. When they're not larking round, the lads love hanging out. And they love their chill time just as much, including getting to go back to their families.

One of the things Directioners love about 1D is how well they get on. The lads seem to love every minute in each other's company and never take their success for granted. Their unbreakable bond, they say, was formed back during the early days of *X Factor* when they were given two weeks to get to know each other before returning to the competition as a band. "We're so lucky that we get on so well," says Louis. "We don't have to work at it at all, it just comes naturally."

Top: In their dressing room at Hall Cross School, Doncaster. **Bottom:** Thankfully Louis only pretend-punched Niall in a Mexico City concert, June 2012.

Top: Waving at fans from their hotel window in Auckland, New Zealand, April 2012. **Bottom:** Chilling back stage at the Patriot Center in Virginia, USA, in 2012.

WITH CELEBRITY FRIENDS

Above: Hanging out with pop music producer and *X Factor* judge Simon Cowell in 2010.

The boys' No. 1 celeb pal? That has to be one Mr Simon Cowell, surely. "I'm so proud of the boys," Simon says. "They've done what so many other British acts want to do and cracked the States." And talking of their global fame, the lads can now count the A-list likes of Katy Perry among their mates – along with home-grown buddies such as Ed Sheeran and The Saturdays. They're even friends with the Prime Minister, David Cameron. Just check out the video for "One Way or Another (Teenage Kicks)" for proof.

Top left: Niall and Liam with singer Alexandra Burke. **Top right:** Harry receives a kiss from Katy Perry at the MTV VMAs in 2012. **Bottom:** One Direction can count the girl group The Saturdays as being celebrity friends.

But who needs celeb friends when you've got mates as good as these? One Direction are true friends on and off stage. Performing in London in 2013, the boys put on a spectacular show for the sell-out audience.

Top left: Perrie Edwards from Little Mix. **Top right:** Harry hanging out with Taylor Swift. **Bottom:** Louis with love of his life Eleanor.

Girls love 1D: 1D love girls. Louis is Mr Commitment and has been dating his lady Eleanor Caldor for ages. Liam was the same before his long-term relationship with dancer Danielle Peazer ended in late 2012. Harry has had numerous short-term flings, including his most famous GFs: pop princess Taylor Swift and TV presenter Caroline Flack. Niall claims to be single but dated student Amy Green in 2012, while Zayn famously hooked up with Little Mix lady Perrie Edwards.

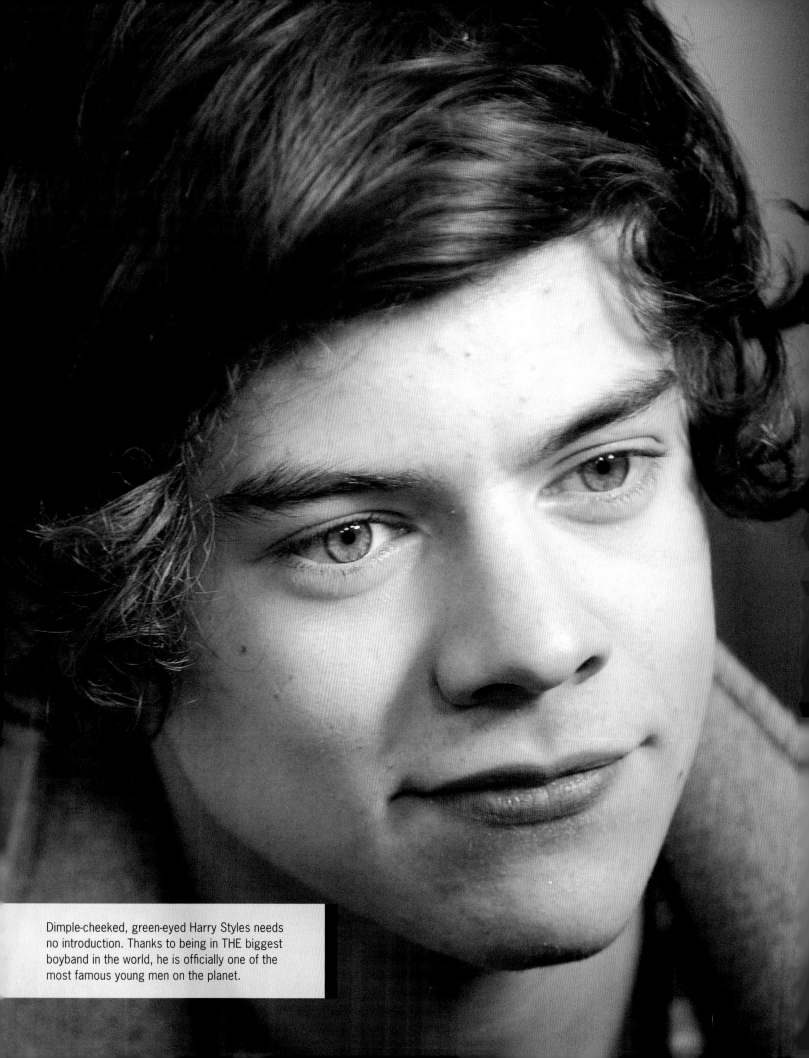

Dimple-cheeked, green-eyed Harry Styles needs no introduction. Thanks to being in THE biggest boyband in the world, he is officially one of the most famous young men on the planet.

HARRY

All-singing, all-performing and all-adorable – Harry is the youngest member of the band and has big ambitions for 1D. He wants them to be as big as The Beatles. 1D have notched up lots of No. 1 albums and singles all across the globe in the space of a few short years, so it's all looking good on that front, Harry!

Singing is not Harry's only passion. He's also a dedicated follower of fashion and loves designer gear. He's gone from high street teen to style icon in just a couple of years and is now a regular on the front row at London catwalk shows. "I like fashion. When I look back at the kind of stuff I wore on the *X Factor*, I laugh," he says.

On stage, Harry rocks a range of looks from preppy to bona fide rock'n'roll star. White tee, skinny jeans, tats. What else does a cool young music god need?

Above: Harry coined the name One Direction during the *X Factor* days – and the name was a lucky one. **Below:** Whether he is smouldering on stage or striking a pose on the red carpet, Harry Styles is a man who lives up to his name.

Harry is the youngest member of the band and was born to folks Anne and Des in 1994 in Holmes Chapel in Cheshire. The charming chappy was destined to capture hearts. When he was little he landed a leading role in his school's big production of *Chitty Chitty Bang Bang*. As a young teen he won a battle of the bands comp and fronted an indie group called White Eskimo – and then, of course, he went on to make the band in the *X Factor*.

Harry loves meeting the fans – even when they embarrass him by producing pictures of him from his childhood.

In a newspaper interview, Harry's dad Des summed up his son's winning appeal: "It's not just his looks but he's very charming, it's like a gift really. I always knew he'd succeed at whatever he did because he'd always charm people… He'd always be able to hold a crowd or hold a room even when he was a kid." Harry certainly knows how to command a crowd and wherever he goes he's met with deafening screams and ladies trying to reach out to touch him.

Squeeeeeeeal! Harry in his trunks on a yacht in Oz! When the boys visited Sydney for the first time in April 2012, they were besieged by fans at the airport and had to sneak out the back door. When they did their first record-store signing they were greeted by screaming fans who'd camped out overnight in the hopes of meeting their idols. No wonder Harry and the boys thoroughly enjoyed some downtime on a swanky yacht in Sydney Harbour in between promo duties.

When Mr Styles and his band mates aren't stripping down to their smalls, they're on stage making audience hearts flutter. Swoon.

1D FEVER!

Above: The One Direction boys hanging out in Sydney in April 2012. **Right:** 1D strike a pose at the Fox TV studios in Australia.

1D are global heart-throbs and world record breakers. When the lads released debut album *Up All Night* it became the fastest-selling debut album in the UK of 2011. It topped the charts in 16 European countries and in Oz. Then, in March 2012, it was released in the States. And the album went off like a firework, entering the charts at No. 1 and making 1D the first-ever British group in chart history to do so. A Guinness World Records entry followed. As did a mass outbreak of 1D fever.

1D took their massively popular *Up All Night Live Tour* to Australia and America in spring and summer of 2012 and were greeted with scenes of fan hysteria. 1D was the name on everyone's lips. When the tour was released on DVD in summer 2012 it topped the charts in 25 countries. Meanwhile, the lads' official book *Dare to Dream: Life as One Direction* topped the UK charts and the *New York Times* Best Seller list. By August 2012, the group's worldwide singles sales exceeded 8 million, while they'd sold 3 million albums and 1 million DVDs.

Top left: Niall on Nova Radio in Oz. **Bottom left:** Performing at the London Olympic Games Closing Ceremony. **Top:** 1D at St Pancras Station, London, in summer 2012. **Bottom:** The boys on tour in Sweden in February 2012.

Top left: 1D performing at the "Today Show" Toyota Concert Series in New York in March 2012. **Bottom left:** At the Beacon Theatre, New York, May 2012. **Above:** Belting out their hits in Melbourne, Australia, in April 2012.

Taking it all in. One Direction's Louis looks from the stage during a performance, coolly drinking in the adulation.

LOUIS

Louis Tomlinson is the oldest member of the band. He was born in 1991 on Christmas Eve and has four sisters to whom he's mega-close. He's the softie and the romantic of the band. When he's not performing or busy promo-ing with 1D, he loves spending time with his girlfriend Eleanor.

Louis is the biggest prankster of the band. He loves joking around in interviews, making the others laugh, doing hilarious impressions and, if the occasion calls for it – like it did in New York at the *Men in Black 3* premiere – pretending to blast the paparazzi with a big plastic toy gun. Louis says, "If I'm going to be stupid and immature, a lot of the time it's with Liam – we've really clicked". You'd never guess Louis' ambition as a kid was to become an actor. Ahem!

Louis looking happy and relaxed in his favourite aviator jacket and stripy tee – Louis's long-term girlfriend Eleanor is a lucky lady!

Whether he's kicking back chilling or out on the road with 1D, Louis' loving fans want constant updates from him – and with almost 10 million followers on Twitter, he's a very popular chappie!

Louis may have millions of followers but he has found that having a massive social media presence has its downsides. "I'm sure if you follow me on Twitter, you'll know that every now and again I'm quite outspoken. I think it's important to speak your mind, and I've had a few rants recently. You know, people who have been horrible to my girlfriend Eleanor and to my mum, and I don't think people should be able to get away with it. I don't go to bed and worry about it: I just think that people, if they want to be like that, should be put in their place." Fair enough!

Sorry, Directioners, Louis only has eyes for his girlfriend Eleanor. And perhaps this koala he met in Sydney in 2012!

Louis loves being on stage and touring the world, but despite the constant screams, No. 1 albums, singles and sell-out tours, the Doncaster fella never lets his feet leave the ground. He says, "At the end of the day we're having a good time. It's almost a cliché but it's so true – if anyone hadn't bought a record we wouldn't be here." One of his favourite places to visit when on tour is Australia. When the band first went Down Under in spring 2012, Louis came face to face with a koala. And he learned to surf. He says, "I just love Australia as a place."

Always wearing the cutest of smiles, here's the super-hot, blue-eyed Louis chilling out in his favourite beanie hat.

One Direction has never been a typical dancing boyband like Take That or Backstreet Boys – and they've never been near a stool like Westlife or Boyz II Men. When the lads' worldwide 2013 tour sold out, Louis was quick to point out that they'd stick with the relaxed stage style. He said, "That's kind of the thing with our shows… We don't dance because we can't dance. Our shows, production-wise, are always quite minimal. We always try and keep it more about us having fun and stay away from gimmicks."

AND THE WINNER IS... 1D!

Above: Victorious! 1D celebrate at the MTV VMAs in Los Angeles in September 2012. **Right:** ID performing on stage at the 2012 MTV VMAs.

1D get almost as many awards flung at them as they do teddies and flowers. They've notched up all the biggies, including three MTV VMAs and a BRIT. Their first bona fide triumph was when they bagged the Best Single BRIT at the 2012 awards for "What Makes You Beautiful". Add to that MTV EMAs, various Billboard awards and two Kids' Choice Awards, and you have quite the haul! "The VMAs is such a prestigious ceremony to play, we were just so honoured," said Liam after the 2012 bash.

Unsurprisingly, 1D are the recipients of a gazillion awards, all the way from A to U in the alphabet. They've won an Aussie ARIA, a German BAMBI, a Japan Gold Disc, a Belgian JIM award, two South American Los Premios awards, a Brazilian MTV award, Brazilian, Mexican, Argentine and UK Nickelodeon awards, a French NRG award, a Radio 1 Teen Award or two, and a UK Music Video Award. Among others.

Left: 1D at the Radio 1 Awards in 2012. **Top:** The boys pose at the BRIT Awards in 2013. **Bottom:** In the press room after scooping their 2012 MTV VMAs.

The world's best boyband, One Direction, showing the crowd what they're made of at the MTV VMAs, September 2012.

In February 2012, the lads became the recipients of the first-ever BRITs Global Success award, launched to reward acts who've notched up mega record and tour sales around the world. There were no other artists who'd scaled anything like the heights scaled by 1D. And yet the humble boys were still gobsmacked to receive their award. "This really is absolutely mind-blowing," Louis said, as the gang accepted it from Robbie Williams.

Left: One Direction at the 2012 BAMBI Awards in Germany.
Bottom left: The boys collecting their Global Success award at the BRITs in 2013. **Below:** 1D on stage the MTV VMAs 2012.

1D TAKE OVER THE WORLD...

Above: The boys hanging out at the Grand Hotel in Stockholm, Sweden. **Right:** 1D rocking in kimonos at Narita International Airport, Japan, January 2013.

At the beginning of 2012, 1D packed their bags and hit Canada and North America to support US band Big Time Rush. They hadn't released a single at this point, yet when they touched down in Canada they brought the country to a standstill. "The fans were chanting our names. They knew the words to the songs off the album that wasn't even out in America," gasped Louis. And when the lads went to Australia and New Zealand, it was the same story. The whole world was falling in love with One Direction...

Above: Harry at a press conference in Tokyo, Japan, in January 2013. **Right:** 1D at a radio station in Sydney, Australia, in April 2012.

When 1D announced their 2013 world tour, in summer 2012, it sold out in minutes flat across the globe. When the lads announced a special one-off gig at New York's historic Madison Square Gardens in December 2012, the same thing happened. The MSG gig was a triumph. Some 18,000 Directioners packed into the atmospheric venue and loved every minute of it. The lads wowed the crowd by belting out insanely catchy hits with big grins on their faces.

Top left: 1D in New York in March 2012.
Bottom left: With their Moonman at the MTV VMAs in September 2012. **Above:** The boys at a *Take Me Home* album promotion in Cologne, Germany, in 2012. **Below:** One Direction performing on Swedish *X Factor* in November 2012.

The lads love travelling the world, meeting fans, promoting their music and appearing on TV and radio stations. One of their most memorable experiences was visiting Tokyo, Japan, at the beginning of 2013. Hundreds of fans turned up at Narita International Airport in Tokyo to meet the lads – and when the band held a press conference they were given traditional Japanese kimonos to wear.

Top left: Performing at the "Today Show" Toyota Concert Series in New York. **Bottom left:** What a doll! The boys with their mini-mes. **Top:** On French NRJ radio show in Paris in February 2012. **Bottom right:** Je t'aime! 1D on French radio station NRJ.

NO STOPPING 1D...

Above: The boys accepting the NRJ Music Award 2012 for Best International Band in Paris. **Right:** 1D performing on their *Take Me Home* Tour in 2013.

Things got off to a roaring start for 1D in 2013. Their Comic Relief single "One Way or Another (Teenage Kicks)" shot to No. 1 in the UK when it was released in February and became the fastest-selling single of the year. The lo-fi vid shows the lads mucking about in London, New York and on tour in Japan. It also shows them hanging out with Ghanaian school kids they met on their Comic Relief trip. "We're just massively honoured to be a part of Comic Relief and we're just loving the fact that we get to do something amazing for such an amazing cause," bubbled Zayn.

And then 1D went 3D. Summer 2013 saw the release of the lads' 3D concert-documentary film, directed by legendary film fella Morgan Spurlock. He was, said the boys' mentor Simon Cowell, "the perfect person to give that access-all-areas, behind-the-scenes look into what it's like to be One Direction today". The lads even got to take it in turns on the camera themselves.

Left: A 1D press conference in Tokyo, Japan, in January 2013. **Above:** Ding, dong 1D on high at the Z100's Jingle Ball Concert in New York, December 2012.

From left to right: Niall: check! Louis: check! Harry: check! Liam and Zayn: check! We all love One Direction.

The boys kicked off their 117-date sell-out *Take Me Home* world tour in early 2013 to massive love. The stages were bigger, the screams louder, yes – but the boys showed they were still the same band we've known and loved all along. The boys laughed, joked and flirted with the fans just as much as they did in their early gigs. Louis explained, "We always try and keep it more about us having fun." And that's the way we love it.

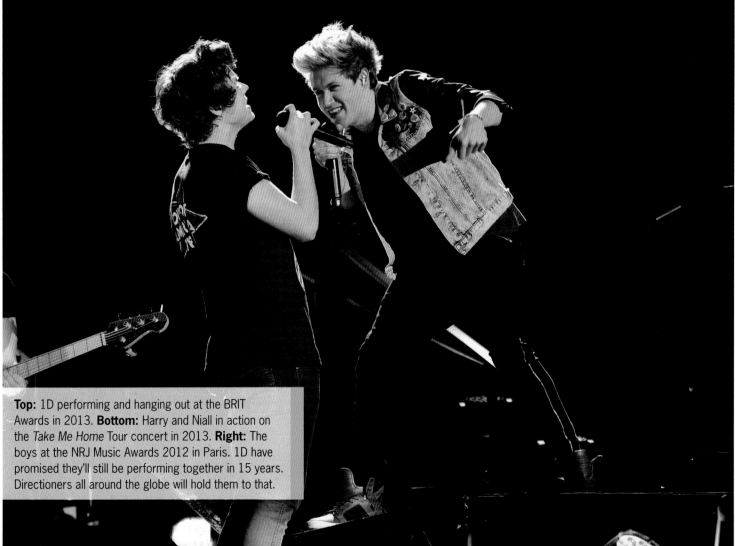

Top: 1D performing and hanging out at the BRIT Awards in 2013. **Bottom:** Harry and Niall in action on the *Take Me Home* Tour concert in 2013. **Right:** The boys at the NRJ Music Awards 2012 in Paris. 1D have promised they'll still be performing together in 15 years. Directioners all around the globe will hold them to that.

CREDITS

The publishers would like to thank Rex Features for their kind permission to reproduce the pictures in this book.

7, 12-13, 17, 22r, 27, 34, 36, 39r, 56, 61tl, 63, 65, 76b; /Action Press: 117t; /Aflo: 40r; /Matt Baron/BEI: 1, 15, 16b, 18, 48t, 62r, 82t, 98, 103t; /Beretta/Sims: 8t, 8b, 19l, 36l, 37, 57b, 61r, 76tl; /Broadimage: 107b; /Rob Cable: 26, 69; /Kristin Callahan: 21, 85b; /Toure Cheick: 119; /Stewart Cook: 44; /Joe Dent: 20, 77; /Everett Collection: 19r; /David Fisher: 2tr, 99, 103l, 107t, 125r, 127b; / Jonathan Hordle: 2br, 82br; /IBL: 58, 91b, 97, 112, 117b; /Sara Jaye: 80r, 123; /Martin Karius: 10t, 91t; /KeystoneUSA-ZUMA: 43, 45b, 90b, 116t; /Julian Makey: 11; /McPix Ltd: 6, 25, 39l, 45t, 45b, 70t, 84; /Curtis Means: 100r; /MediaPunch: 38, 52, 66, 70b, 78, 87; / Most Wanted: 110t; /Eddie Mulholland: 10b; /Newspix: 42, 86, 100; /Niviere/Sipa: 120; /NTI Media Ltd: 72; /Masatoshi Okauchi: 113, 114, 122; /Erik Pendzich: 60; /PictureGroup 2tl, 35, 53, 54-55, 73tr, 104, 105, 107-108, 111, 127t, 128; /Picture Perfect: 41, 118t; / QMI Agency: 46b; /Brian Rasic: 5, 27t, 30t, 30b, 49, 85t, 94, 106, 110b; /Paul Richardson: 23, 57t, 124l, 125c, 125r; /Nathan Richter/ Newspix: 101; /Nancy Rivera: 68; /Marc Robertson/Newspix: 64; /David Rowland: 59, 71t; /Willi Schneider: 80l; /Jason Sheldon: 24; /Jim Smeal: 2bl, 40l; /Startraks Photo: 22l, 50, 61b, 76tr, 81, 92t, 95, 96t; /Graham Stone: 62l; /Owen Sweeney: 16t; /Charles Sykes: 102; / Hugh Thompson: 28-29; /Vivid: 118b; /Richard Young: 37, 73tl, 73b, 82bl, 83, 100b, 126t; /Toby Zerna/Newspix: 67, 88, 90t

Additional photographs: 14, 32, 46-47, 74-75, 121, 126b Corbis/James Whatling/Splash/Splash News

Every effort has been made to acknowledge correctly and contact the source and/or copyright holder of each picture and Carlton Books Limited apologizes for any unintentional errors or omissions, which will be corrected in future editions of this book.

First published in 2013 by
Carlton Books
Carlton Publishing Group
20 Mortimer Street
London W1T 3JW

Text and design copyright © Carlton Books Limited 2013

A CIP catalogue record for this book is available from the British Library.
ISBN 978-1-78097-415-6
Printed and bound in Dubai